They who trust with faith un - shak - en By their God are
He who ev - er gent - ly schools me, He who dai - ly
I shall strive to win a trea - sure That will bring me
To His lov - ing - kind - ness ten - der Soul and bod - y

not for - sak - en And will keep a daunt - less heart.
guides and rules me Will re - main my help di - vine.
last - ing plea - sure And that now is sel - dom found.
I sur - ren - der, For on God a - lone I build.

Text: *Andächtige Haus-Kirche,* 1676, Nürnberg;
tr. Catherine Winkworth, 1827–78, alt.
Tune: ALLES IST AN GOTTES SEGEN, Johann Löhner, 1645–1705;
adapt. Johann Balthasar König, 1691–1758

THE NARRATION AND TABLEAU

INTRODUCTION

1. Now and then, we all like to stop and review our lives. We remember both the happy and the unpleasant experiences we have had. Some of these happenings have changed our lives more than others. All our experiences have helped to make us who we are today. By God's grace, many of our experiences will be God's instruments for drawing us closer to Him.

2. People have had much to do with shaping our lives. God has used those closest to us—our friends, parents, brothers, sisters, relatives, and friends—to help mold us. He has also used those far from us, both living and dead, to help make us the persons that we are.

3. Now let us go back in history about 500 years. We will look at some of the people, places, and events that changed Martin Luther's life. As we view these scenes, we will see them also as moments in history that had a great influence on each of us, in one way or another, for Luther was used by God to speak to our time as well as his own.

PART I

OCTOBER 31, 1517—THE NINETY-FIVE THESES

4. Popes had been selling indulgences long before Luther's time. The Roman Catholic Church taught that these indulgences forgave the temporal punishments people had earned by sinning. These punishments, many people believed, would take place either on earth or in purgatory, a place of suffering between heaven and hell.

5. People believed that one way of escaping much, or even all, of this suffering was to do good works. Another way to escape this suffering was to buy the extra good works of the saints. An indulgence, then, was a way for the pope to

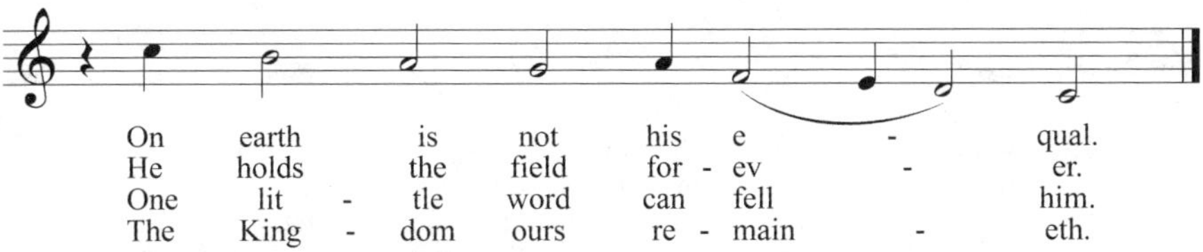

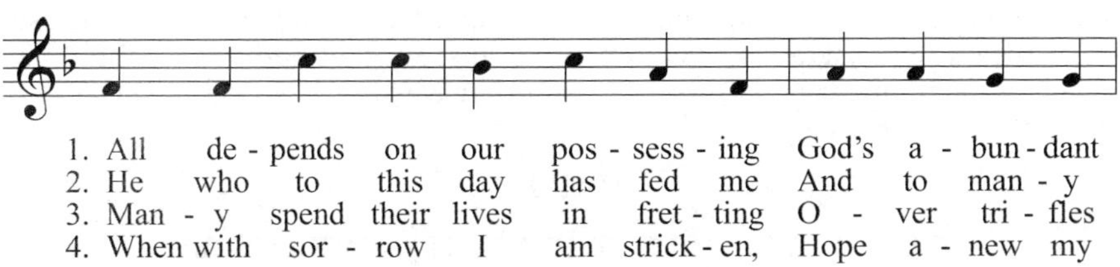

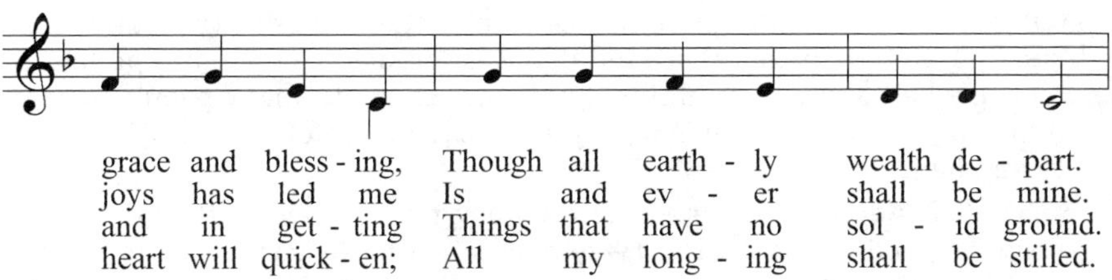

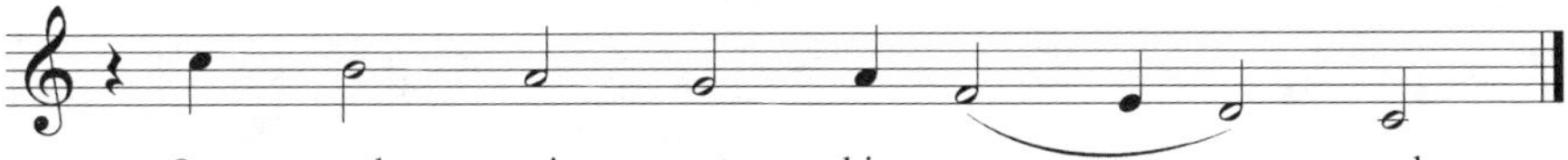

On earth is not his e - qual.
He holds the field for - ev - er.
One lit - tle word can fell him.
The King - dom ours re - main - eth.

Text: Martin Luther, 1483–1546; tr. composite
Tune: EIN FESTE BURG, Martin Luther, 1483–1546
Text and tune: Public domain

THE VERSICLES AND GLORIA PATRI

LEADER: O Lord, open my lips,
CONGREGATION: **and my mouth will declare Your praise.** *Psalm 51:15*
LEADER: Make haste, O God, to deliver me;
CONGREGATION: **make haste to help me, O Lord.** *Psalm 70:1*

Glory be to the Father and to the Son and to the Holy Spirit; as it was in the beginning, is now, and will be forever. Amen. Praise to You, O Christ. Alleluia.

PSALM 47

THE SCRIPTURE LESSON *Galatians 2:16–21* or *John 2:13–17*

THE ANTHEM *The Choir*

THE HOMILY

THE OFFERING

THE HYMN OF FAITH

"All Depends on Our Possessing" *LSB* 732:1–4 *The Congregation*

All Depends on Our Possessing

1. All de - pends on our pos - sess - ing God's a - bun - dant
2. He who to this day has fed me And to man - y
3. Man - y spend their lives in fret - ting O - ver tri - fles
4. When with sor - row I am strick - en, Hope a - new my

grace and bless - ing, Though all earth - ly wealth de - part.
joys has led me Is and ev - er shall be mine.
and in get - ting Things that have no sol - id ground.
heart will quick - en; All my long - ing shall be stilled.

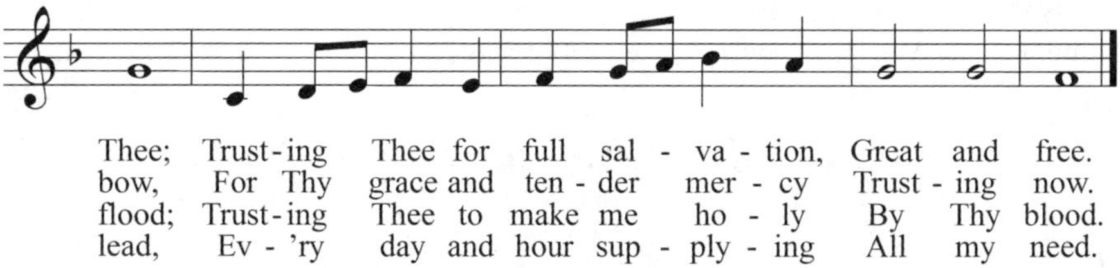

Great Days *in the Life of* Luther

A Reformation Worship Service with Tableaux for Children and Adults

CONCORDIA PUBLISHING HOUSE • SAINT LOUIS

THE PRELUDE

THE REFORMATION HYMN

"A Mighty Fortress Is Our God" *LSB* 656 *The Congregation*

A Mighty Fortress Is Our God

Text: Martin Luther, 1483–1546; tr. composite
Tune: EIN FESTE BURG, Martin Luther, 1483–1546
Text and tune: Public domain

THE VERSICLES AND GLORIA PATRI

LEADER: O Lord, open my lips,

CONGREGATION: and my mouth will declare Your praise. *Psalm 51:15*

LEADER: Make haste, O God, to deliver me;

CONGREGATION: make haste to help me, O Lord. *Psalm 70:1*

Glory be to the Father and to the Son and to the Holy Spirit;
as it was in the beginning, is now, and will be forever. Amen.
Praise to You, O Christ. Alleluia.

PSALM 47

THE SCRIPTURE LESSON *Galatians 2:16–21* or *John 2:13–17*

THE ANTHEM *The Choir*

THE HOMILY

THE OFFERING

THE HYMN OF FAITH

"All Depends on Our Possessing" *LSB* 732:1–4 *The Congregation*

All Depends on Our Possessing

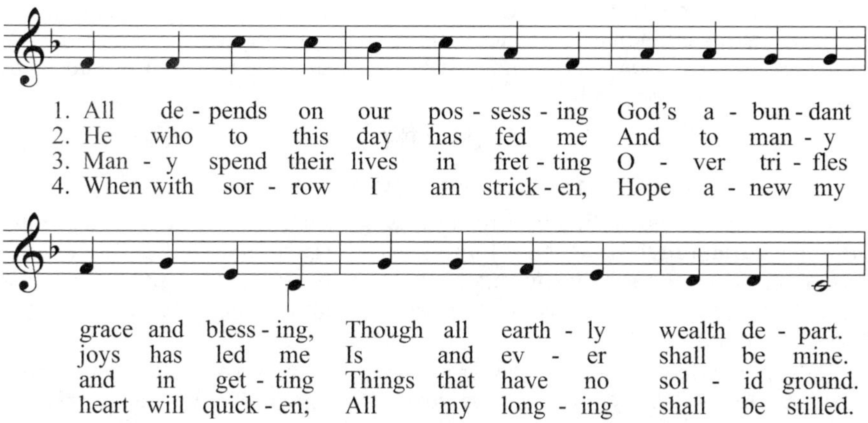

Text: *Andächtige Haus-Kirche,* 1676, Nürnberg;
tr. Catherine Winkworth, 1827–78, alt.
Tune: ALLES IST AN GOTTES SEGEN, Johann Löhner, 1645–1705;
adapt. Johann Balthasar König, 1691–1758
Text and music: Public domain

THE NARRATION AND TABLEAU

INTRODUCTION

1. Now and then, we all like to stop and review our lives. We remember both the happy and the unpleasant experiences we have had. Some of these happenings have changed our lives more than others. All our experiences have helped to make us who we are today. By God's grace, many of our experiences will be God's instruments for drawing us closer to Him.

2. People have had much to do with shaping our lives. God has used those closest to us—our friends, parents, brothers, sisters, relatives, and friends—to help mold us. He has also used those far from us, both living and dead, to help make us the persons that we are.

3. Now let us go back in history about 500 years. We will look at some of the people, places, and events that changed Martin Luther's life. As we view these scenes, we will see them also as moments in history that had a great influence on each of us, in one way or another, for Luther was used by God to speak to our time as well as his own.

PART I

OCTOBER 31, 1517—THE NINETY-FIVE THESES

4. Popes had been selling indulgences long before Luther's time. The Roman Catholic Church taught that these indulgences forgave the temporal punishments people had earned by sinning. These punishments, many people believed, would take place either on earth or in purgatory, a place of suffering between heaven and hell.

5. People believed that one way of escaping much, or even all, of this suffering was to do good works. Another way to escape this suffering was to buy the extra good works of the saints. An indulgence, then, was a way for the pope to

transfer the good works of saints to another person. This transfer was usually made after money had been paid to the church.

6. Unfortunately, many people did not understand what these indulgences were really supposed to do—transfer good works. Many people mistakenly thought they received forgiveness for all their sins when they purchased an indulgence.

7. In 1517, a friar named John Tetzel was sent to areas near Wittenberg to sell indulgences. Martin Luther, who lived and taught in Wittenberg, heard about this. He also noticed that many people thought they were buying forgiveness of sins.

8. These reports disturbed Luther very much. He preached about indulgences in his sermons. "He who does not believe on the Lord Jesus will be condemned," Luther said. "The wicked must forsake sinful ways," he warned.

9. Many people, however, continued to believe that they could buy forgiveness of sins and that they did not have to change their evil ways. Some of the members of Luther's church told him they no longer needed to come to church—their sins were forgiven because they had bought an indulgence.

10. Luther decided to try another way to convince the people that purchasing indulgences did not bring forgiveness of sins. He decided to hold a public debate and discussion on the subject. He would ask others to discuss whether Tetzel's way of selling indulgences for the forgiveness of sins was right.

11. Our first close view into Luther's life takes us to Wittenberg, Germany. It is October 31, 1517.

SCENE 1

(Organ or band music may be played to provide time for those in the tableau to reach their places; Luther and townspeople enter.)

NARRATOR:

Luther rises early this morning.

He delivers two lectures at the University of Wittenberg.

From the university, he walks to the monastery.

In a large study room, he puts the finishing touches on the Ninety-Five Theses, or statements, he plans to use in his debate on the sale of indulgences by the pope.

His writing finished, he leaves the monastery and walks toward the Castle Church, accompanied by one or two students.

At the door of the church, Luther stops. He nails the Ninety-Five Theses and the invitation to debate on the door. He leaves quietly.

(Organ or band music plays while tableau characters exit.)

12. This almost unnoticed event seemed unimportant at the time. From that moment on, however, the whole world would be changed. These theses soon exploded like bombshells among those who bought and sold indulgences and among those who had led the church into false ways.

13. Thesis 1: "When our Lord and Master Jesus Christ said, 'Repent,' He wanted the entire life of believers to be one of repentance."

14. Thesis 10: "Those priests act ignorantly and wickedly who, in the case of the dying, reserve canonical penalties for purgatory."

15. Thesis 32: "Those who believe that they can be certain of their salvation because they have indulgence letters will be eternally damned, together with their teachers."

16. Thesis 62: "The true treasure of the church is the most holy Gospel of the glory and grace of God."

17. Thesis 94: "Christians should be exhorted to be diligent in following Christ, their head, through penalties, death, and hell."

THE HYMN OF TRUST

"How Firm a Foundation" *LSB* 728
Stanzas 1, 3, 5—*Congregation and Children;*
stanza 2—*Children;* stanza 4—*Choir*

How Firm a Foundation

Text: *A Selection of Hymns*, London, 1787, alt.
Tune: FOUNDATION, *Genuine Church Music*, Winchester, 1832
Text and tune: Public domain

PART II

DECEMBER 10, 1520—THE BURNING OF THE PAPAL BULL

18. From 1517 to 1520, Luther publicly denounced some of the other church practices that hid the good news of the Gospel of forgiveness of sins through Jesus. He tried to show the people and the leaders of the church that many of the things being taught in the church did not agree with the Bible.

19. Dr. John Eck, one of the pope's German supporters, debated some of these issues with Luther at Heidelberg in the spring of 1518. Their debate lasted fourteen days. During this time, Dr. Eck was not able to convince Luther that he was wrong.

20. Luther stuck to the truths he had found in the Word of God. "The Law of God is not able to bring man to righteousness. The Law says, 'Do this!' and it is never done. Grace says, 'Believe in this man (Jesus)!' and immediately it is done."

21. Four months after the debate, Dr. Eck went to see the pope in Rome. When Eck returned to Germany, he brought with him a document, a papal bull, with the papal seal on it.

22. The papal bull stated that Luther's writings must be burned. It also commanded Luther to take back all he had written and said if Luther would not do this within sixty days, he would be accursed and properly punished; he would be cut off from church membership and all church privileges.

23. Luther ignored the pope's bull. Many others ignored it also. University students made fun of it. Public opposition prevented it from being published in Wittenberg.

24. This decree disturbed some of Luther's friends, however. They advised Luther to take back what he had said and written. He refused. Let us look in on the events of December 10, 1520.

SCENE II

(Organ or band music plays while the characters take their places; Luther, students, and townspeople enter.)

NARRATOR:

One of Luther's friends posts a special announcement on the university bulletin board. It reads: "All professors, students, and townspeople are invited to meet just outside the east gate of Wittenberg at 9:00 a.m. Here the false teachings of the church will be burned."

The crowd gathers. Soon, Luther arrives. One of the professors lights the bonfire. Book after book is thrown into the flames.

Suddenly, Luther takes from his gown a copy of the papal bull. He steps forward and throws it into the fire! He is heard to say: "Because you have destroyed the truth of God, may the Lord consume you in these flames."

(Introduce the hymn as all exit.)

THE HYMN OF CONSECRATION

"Jesus, I My Cross Have Taken" (stanzas 1–3, 6) Tune: *LSB* 700

Stanzas 1, 6—*Congregation and Children;* stanza 2—*Children;* stanza 3—*Choir*

Jesus, I My Cross Have Taken

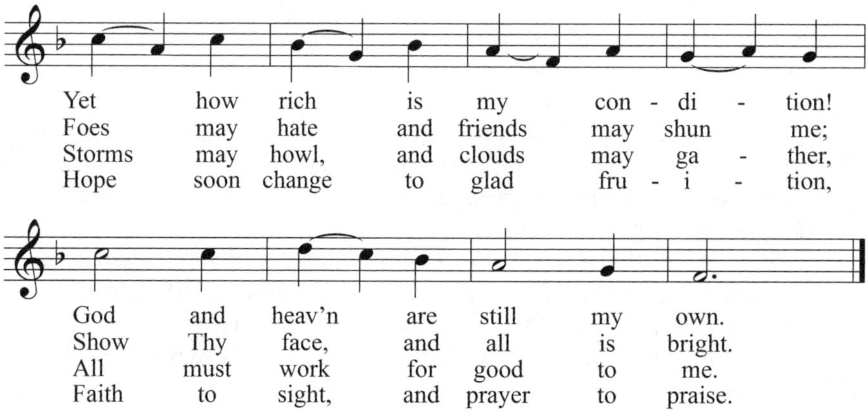

Text: Henry Francis Lyte, 1793–1847, abr., alt.
Tune: HYFRYDOL, Rowland H. Prichard, 1811–87
Text and music: Public domain

THE NARRATION AND TABLEAU

PART III

APRIL 18, 1521—THE DIET OF WORMS

25. Charles V was emperor of the Holy Roman Empire. Many important matters in his empire had to be settled, so a meeting, or assembly, known as a diet, was scheduled in the city of Worms.

26. The most important question was the disagreement between the pope and Martin Luther. Many members of the diet wanted the emperor to give Luther a trial before sentencing him. The emperor finally agreed and sent Luther a letter promising protection for the journey from Wittenberg to Worms.

27. The emperor's herald called for Luther at Wittenberg. A monk, a husky student, and a personal friend of Luther also joined the travelers. The city of Wittenberg gave the group some expense money, and a friend loaned them his carriage.

28. As Luther approached the towns along the route to Worms, the people ran out to meet him. They wanted to see this hero who was brave enough to oppose the pope and what seemed like the whole world.

29. Most people were sure that Luther was going to his doom. They remembered how John Hus had been burned at the stake. Luther's response was, "Indeed, Christ is alive, and I shall enter Worms in spite of the gates of hell and the powers of darkness."

30. We look back, then, on the city of Worms. It is the afternoon of April 17, 1521.

SCENE III

(Organ or band music plays as soldiers, princes, emperor, guard, Luther, and townspeople enter.)

NARRATOR:

Large crowds have gathered in the streets. The herald leads Luther through the back streets to the meeting hall of the diet. Finally, Luther stands before the majestic gathering of bishops, princes, electors, a representative of the pope, and Emperor Charles V.

An officer tells Luther, "Speak only when you are asked a question."

The chairman reads the titles of Luther's books and pamphlets. The chairman then asks, "Did you write these?" Luther admits he did. "Yes."

Then, Luther hears this question: "Will you recant, or take back, the false teachings in your writings?"

Luther cannot answer this question without more careful consideration. He asks permission to give his answer tomorrow.

After spending the night in serious, prayerful thought, Luther's answer comes loud and clear. He explains, "My writings are of three kinds.

1. First are those that deal with the blessings of faith and good order.

2. Next are those that were written against the pope and his followers.

3. Last are those that were written against individuals who had taught falsely."

He finishes by saying, "I can withdraw none of them."

Then, the chairman asks Luther to answer more definitely. Luther speaks:

"Since I am held captive by the Scriptures which I have quoted, and my conscience is bound by them, therefore I cannot and will not recant, because to deal against conscience is a dangerous thing. God help me. Amen."

(Introduce the hymn as all exit.)

THE HYMN OF FORGIVENESS

"I Am Trusting Thee, Lord Jesus" *LSB* 729:1–4 *The Younger Children*

I Am Trusting Thee, Lord Jesus

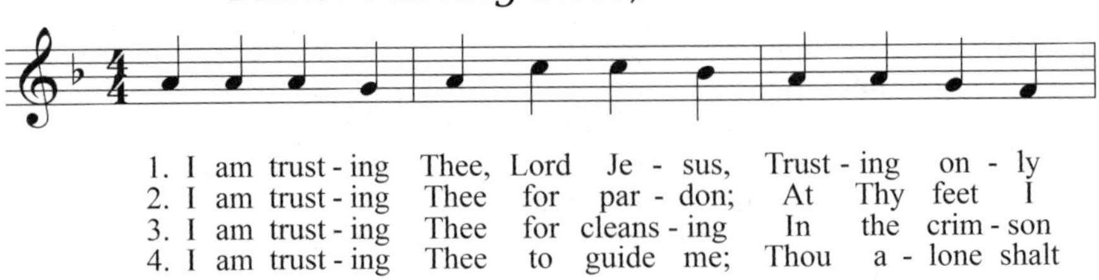

Thee; Trust-ing Thee for full sal - va - tion, Great and free.
bow, For Thy grace and ten - der mer - cy Trust - ing now.
flood; Trust-ing Thee to make me ho - ly By Thy blood.
lead, Ev - 'ry day and hour sup - ply - ing All my need.

Text: Frances R. Havergal, 1836–79
Tune: STEPHANOS, Henry W. Baker, 1821–77
Text and tune: Public domain

THE NARRATION AND TABLEAU

PART IV

MAY 4, 1521—WARTBURG CASTLE

31. After Luther's statement at Worms, his life was in serious danger. Luther's prince and friend, Frederick of Saxony, had secretly worked out a plan to protect Luther.

32. Luther left Worms for Wittenberg on April 26, 1521. He preached sermons and visited relatives on the way. Then, late in the evening of May 4, while his group was traveling through the forest, Luther was captured by a band of armed men.

33. His friends were allowed to continue their journey, but he was given knight's clothing to wear, put on a horse, and taken by little-known paths to the Wartburg castle. Here, he was kept safe from harm.

34. Few people knew where Luther was. Even Prince Frederick did not know. Only the captain of the guard at the castle knew who the prisoner really was.

35. In the meantime, Emperor Charles ordered that no one in the empire should help or protect Luther. No one was to house him or feed him. His books were not to be printed, sold, or read.

36. We look in on Luther again. This time, it is hard to recognize him. He has grown a beard, and people call him Knight George.

SCENE IV

(Organ or band music plays as Luther, dressed as a knight with a beard, and an assistant enter.)

NARRATOR:

Luther has his own room in Wartburg castle. Here, he lives a quiet, protected, but very busy and productive life.

He continues to write one pamphlet after another. In some, he defends himself; in others, he makes new attacks on false teachings. He works on sermon helps for pastors. "I intend to stay here until Easter," he wrote. "In the meantime, I intend to prepare the postils and translate the New Testament into the language of the people."

In about eleven weeks, he translates the whole New Testament into the German language. Thousands of copies are printed and sold during the next years.

(Introduce the hymn as both exit.)

THE HYMN OF INVITATION

"'Come, Follow Me,' the Savior Spake" *LSB* 688:1–3 *The Congregation and Children*

"Come, Follow Me," the Savior Spake

Text: Johann Scheffler, 1624–77, sts. 1–3; tr. Charles W. Schaeffer, 1813–96
Tune: MACHS MIT MIR, GOTT; Bartholomäus Gesius, c. 1555–1613, adapt.

CLOSING

37. Early in 1522, Luther returned to Wittenberg, even though he was still in danger. Until his death in 1546, he continued to live a productive and dramatic life.

38. Still today, people continue to be amazed at the great number of writings of Martin Luther. At times, he was very sick, yet he wrote, he taught, he preached, he traveled, he debated. We need not be surprised that he could do so much, for all his life he relied on God for strength and wisdom.

39. He wrote the catechisms, but more important, he prayed the catechism. He studied God's Word, not only so he could translate, write, and preach, but also so he could be nurtured by God's Word. He longed to hear the good news of the Gospel. He wanted to explore every aspect of the message that God had declared him righteous because Jesus had died for him and rose again.

40. Luther's life has made our lives different from what they otherwise would have been. We, too, have the Bible in our own language. In our own time, people are translating the Bible into more languages. Our church services are conducted in our own language.

41. Education for all is common. Lutheran churches operate schools, Sunday Schools, and Vacation Bible Schools. They have Bible classes so people can study God's Word and be strengthened by the Gospel.

42. Because Martin Luther, by God's grace, rediscovered that by grace and by faith in Christ alone we are saved, we can come to God, confident that we are His own. May the Holy Spirit help each of us come to the Lord with such faith.

THE HYMN OF DEVOTION

"Take My Life and Let It Be" *LSB* 783

Stanzas 1, 2, 4, and 6—*Congregation and Children;* stanza 3—*Children;* stanza 5—*Choir*

Take My Life and Let It Be

5. Take my will and make it Thine,
It shall be no longer mine;
Take my heart, it is Thine own,
It shall be Thy royal throne.

6. Take my love, my Lord, I pour
At Thy feet its treasure store;
Take myself, and I will be
Ever, only, all for Thee.

Text: Frances R. Havergal, 1836–79
Tune: PATMOS; William H. Havergal, 1793–1870
Text and tune: Public domain

THE PRAYERS

THE BENEDICTION

THE POSTLUDE

NOTES TO THE LEADER

The following suggestions are offered as guidelines. Those who use this service should adapt and change it to fit local conditions.

Psalm 47: Psalm 47 may be sung responsively by pastor and children, or by pastor and congregation, or by children and congregation. It may also be chanted by a choir or group of children. The antiphon should be sung first by a soloist or small group and then repeated by the congregation before the first section of the psalm is sung.

The Anthem: The anthem may be any appropriate chorale sung by a choir or group of children.

The Narration: The numbered narrations may be read from a lectern or reading stand by individual children. They may be read wholly or in part from another part of the church (for example, a balcony or in the main aisle of the church) or over a public-address system. Some parts may be selected for choral reading. The sections marked "Narrator" could be read by one or more adults, or they could be divided up and read by children to provide more speaking parts.

The Tableau: Characters may be changed as seems necessary. With more space, more characters may be included. The large-group members are not to act. They go to their assigned places and remain steady and quiet while the narration is read. Main characters should act out those parts described in each scene. They should speak the parts in quotation marks.

Scene I—Luther is followed by townspeople. They proceed to front of chancel. Luther is dressed in his black doctor's gown. He carries a large paper representing the Ninety-Five Theses. Townspeople wear German folk costumes: shawls, full skirts (women); tight trousers, long full sleeves (men).

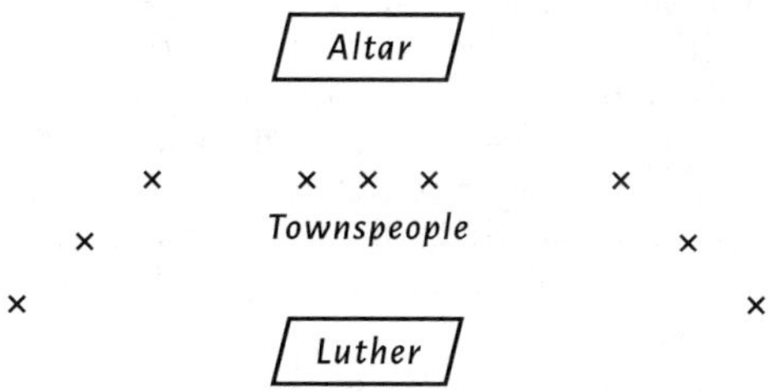

Scene II—Luther, carrying large books, is followed by a group of students. Townspeople follow some distance behind. Luther wears a black gown; the townspeople, folk costumes; the students, long, plain gowns with wide, tight cloth belts.

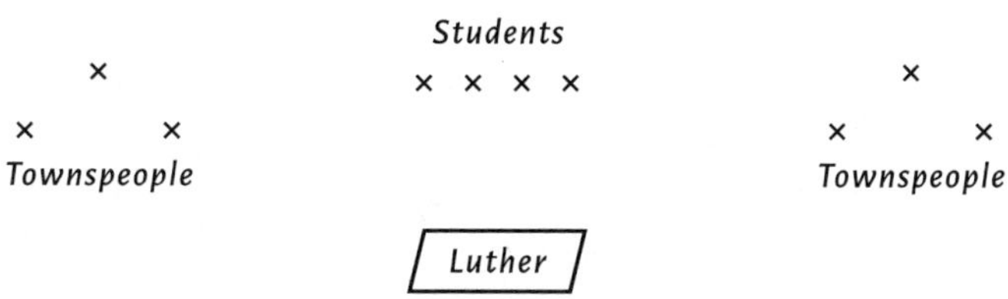

Scene III—Soldiers, princes, and the emperor enter, followed by a guard, Luther, and several townspeople. Luther wears a black gown. Emperor and princes are dressed in colorful royal garb. Soldiers carry spears. Guard holds chains.

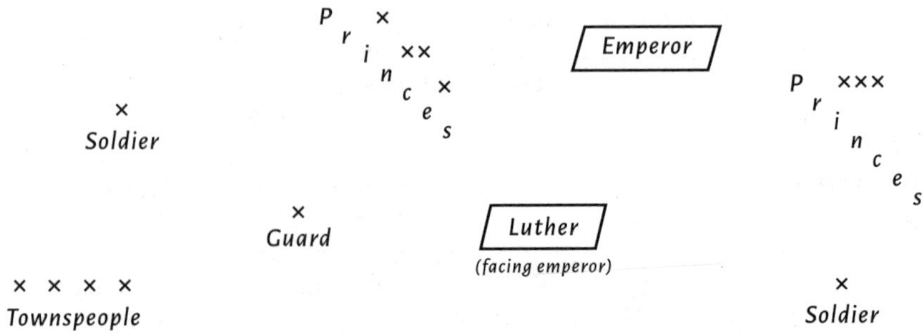

Scene IV—Luther and assistant wear black gowns. Assistant holds books, writing quill. They face each other; both hold a large open book.

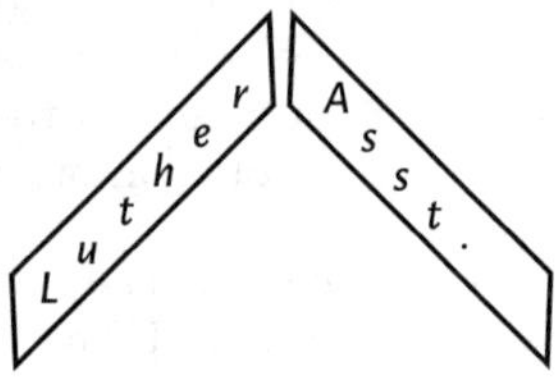

Music—Organ or band music should accompany the movement of characters to and from their positions. Use variations on one theme, such as the chorale "A Mighty Fortress Is Our God." An organ intonation that is used to introduce each hymn may serve as the music that allows scene changes. Guide your students in writing an appropriate prayer or two that could be used at the conclusion of your presentation. Ask your pastor to prepare a brief homily, conduct the opening service, and give the Benediction. Use your student musicians as much as possible in this presentation.

May the Lord bless your efforts to teach and tell the story of the Reformation and the blessings of the Gospel that God brought to the church through His servant Martin Luther.